Tex ve the Nightmare

Written by Lindsay Galvin
Illustrated by Juanbjuan Oliver

Collins

1 Bedtime

Tex and his older brother Rohan share bunkbeds. Tex always likes to talk for as long as possible before he goes to sleep.

"Let's imagine our bed is a spaceship, off to visit a distant planet," says Tex.

Rohan yawns. "Tomorrow, Tex. Turn out the light. I'm going to sleep now."

"No! You can't sleep – you're the captain and the spaceship will crash and —"

Rohan is soon snoring like an aeroplane taking off. He always falls straight to sleep.

Tex feels really sleepy, too. He turns off the light, but tries to keep his eyes open, because he knows what will happen when he falls asleep.

The nightmare.

Soon, it is too late. Tex can't keep awake.

2 The nightmare vs Tex

Tex hears a knocking on the wardrobe door. He is filled with dread and wants to hide under the covers.

Instead, he finds himself climbing out of bed, then his hand is on the wardrobe door handle, pulling …

A giant purple hairy monster leaps out of the wardrobe, with claws out and teeth on show ...

Tex wakes up panting, with the covers tangled around him. He switches on his lamp, staring at the wardrobe door.

He listens to his brother's snoring and feels a bit better.

Tex gets up and forces himself to open the wardrobe door. The only monstrous thing inside is a monstrous pile of clothes.

So why does he still feel scared?

Tex tries to think of nice things like swimming at the beach on holiday and the smell of fresh bread at the bakery. It helps him to relax but it still takes him a long time to fall back to sleep.

3 Rohan's nightmare

At breakfast, Tex is too tired to eat his toast.

"If you're not eating that, I'll have it," says Rohan. Tex shrugs and yawns.

Rohan stares at him. "Did you have a nightmare again? You know you don't have to put up with those bullying dreams."

"I don't have much choice when I'm asleep," says Tex.

"I once scared away a nightmare crow the size of a car, pecking at the window!" claims Rohan.

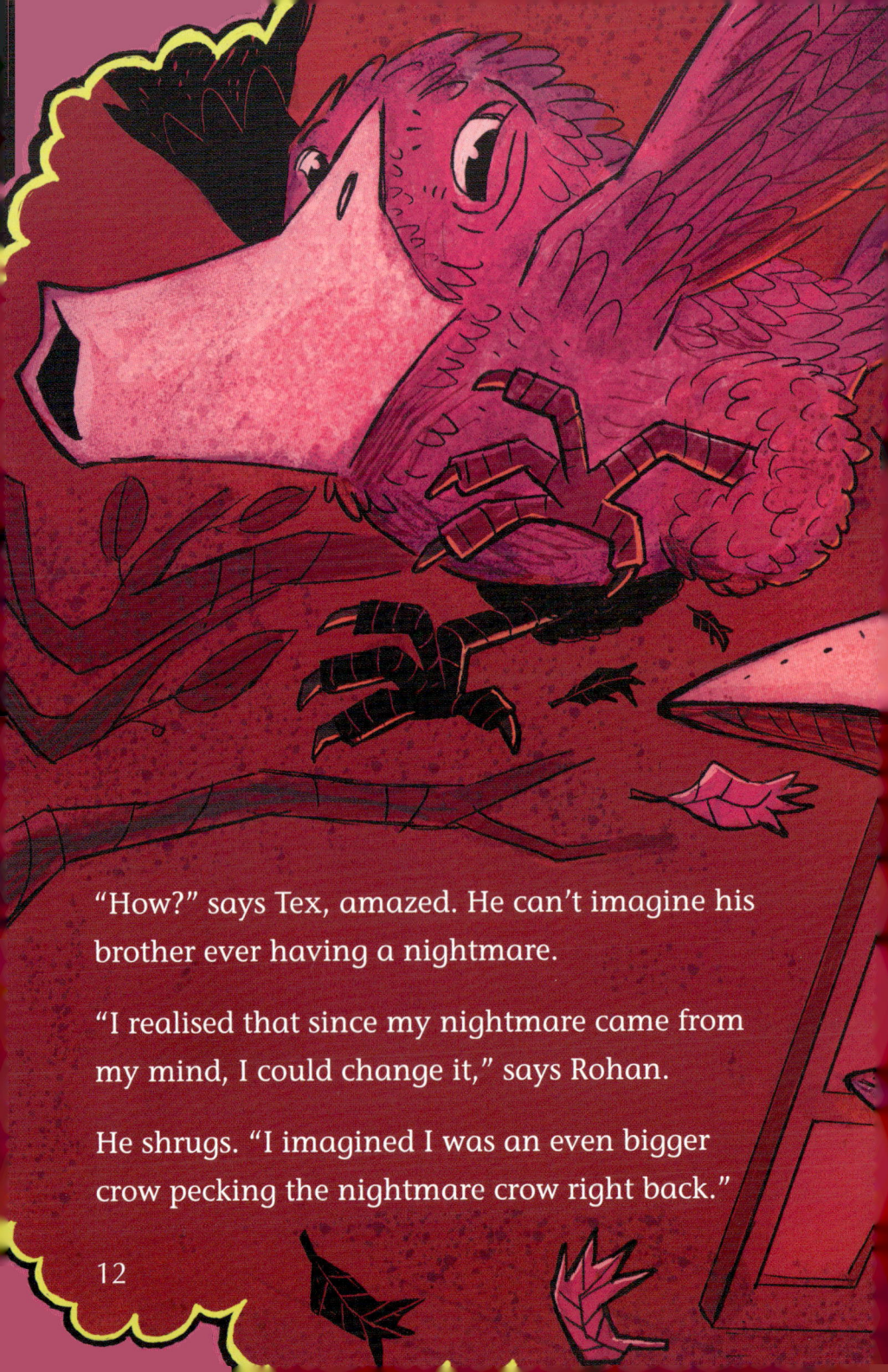

"How?" says Tex, amazed. He can't imagine his brother ever having a nightmare.

"I realised that since my nightmare came from my mind, I could change it," says Rohan.

He shrugs. "I imagined I was an even bigger crow pecking the nightmare crow right back."

"Did you ever have the nightmare again?" asks Tex.

"I did, but the next time I half woke up and remembered I was a boss level king crow. That ordinary giant crow wasn't messing with me. There was an epic fight and I won, of course."

"Because it was your own mind," says Tex.

"Exactly," says Rohan.

4 The plan

At school, Tex remembers what Rohan told him. How can he defeat an enormous hairy purple monster?

He waves his pencil.

What if he had a laser pencil and zapped it? He could shrink it. Zap!

Tex's tummy rumbles, reminding him to eat his snack.

What if the monster is grumpy because it is hungry?

Maybe he needs to distract it with some toast.

He sighs. He wishes Rohan could be in his dream. He would know what to do.

That night, Tex is so tired that he falls asleep quickly.

The nightmare is waiting.

Tex opens the wardrobe door. The monster seems even hairier and scarier, eyes glowing, teeth glinting …

Tex wakes up, terrified.

He remembers he has a plan to defeat the nightmare.

Tex forces himself to not turn on the light. He listens to Rohan's snoring and closes his eyes, reminding himself that this is his mind and he's in charge.

The nightmare is back.

The wardrobe opens. Seeing the monster scares Tex so much that he almost forgets the plan.

Then, all of a sudden, he's holding the laser pencil in one hand and a piece of toast in the other.

5 Tex vs the nightmare

Deep in his nightmare, Tex is now armed with the laser pencil and the toast.

But the monster is so scary, he panics and can't remember the plan. What was the laser supposed to do?

The laser pencil accidentally zaps the toast. Instead of shrinking, the slice of toast grows huge, sprouting arms, legs and teeth, and runs towards Rohan.

This is even worse than before!

With a boy-eating toast slice about to eat his brother, Tex forgets all about the monster, who is now creeping up behind him.

Tex spins around and gasps.

The monster leaps right over him and gobbles the overgrown toast in two big bites. It rubs its tummy and grins. "Thank you," it says.

The next morning at breakfast, Tex tucks into his toast. He smiles to himself as he remembers the monster in the nightmare doing the same. The monster was just hungry. Everyone gets grumpy when they're hungry.

He changed his nightmare, even if it didn't quite go as planned.

"It looks like you had a good night's sleep," says Rohan.

Tex finishes his toast and licks his fingers. "Actually, I did in the end," he replies.

He quickly steals Rohan's slice of toast and takes an extra big bite.

Tex's emotions

excited

relieved

terrified

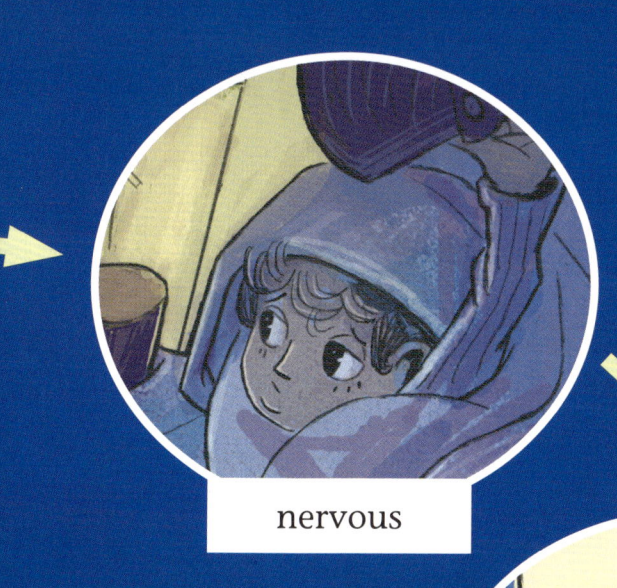
nervous

scared

hopeful

 Ideas for reading

Written by Gill Matthews
Primary Literacy Consultant

Reading objectives:
- discuss the sequence of events in books and how items of information are related
- discuss and clarify the meanings of words, linking new meanings to known vocabulary
- make inferences on the basis of what is being said and done
- predict what might happen on the basis of what has been read so far

Spoken language objectives:
- articulate and justify answers, arguments and opinions
- participate in discussions, presentations, performances, role play, improvisations and debates

Curriculum links: Relationships Education: Families and people who care for me

Interest words: dread, panting, relax, defeat

Word count: 873

Build a context for reading

- Ask children to look closely at the front cover of the book and to read the title.
- Explore their understanding of the words *versus* and *nightmare*.
- Ask what they think Tex's nightmare might be about.
- Encourage children to talk about their dreams – both good and bad and why they think people dream.
- Read the back cover blurb. Ask what they think is going to happen in the story.

Understand and apply reading strategies

- Read pp2–5 aloud, using punctuation, dialogue and meaning to help you read with appropriate expression.
- Discuss why Tex is trying to stay awake. Encourage children to support their ideas with reasons and evidence.